How To Curse Enemies For Real

Crafty Witch

Is someone standing in your way? Stopping you from achieving your dreams or getting everything your heart desires?

When all other avenues fail, you can use dark magic to bring about the outcome you require.

If you want to learn how to use black magic to change the course of your future, keep reading.....

Contents:

Passion On Your Doorstep

Double Poppets

Money Enchantment

Make Me Spell

Stand Tall

Pour On Protection

Floor Wash Lover

Romance Doll

Root Of Love

Light Of Love

Bad Luck Locked In

In The Dead Of Night

Apple Sweet Enchantment

Your Heart Be Mine

The Joining Of Two Spell

Boiling Rage

Bottled Belladonna

Covet Candle

Descending Ailments

Reflect Your Revenge

Black Moon Revenge

Peppered Pentacle

Curse Of The Rocky Road

Snake Eyes

Dark Embrace

Shaddow Whispers

Banishing Mirror

Freeze Out Your Foe

The Banishing Jar

- Witch Bottle
- Home Security
- Herbal Shield
- Deflect Harm
- Vinegar Turnaround
- Psychic Shield
- Unbreakable Shield
- Blocked And Locked
- Deflection Reflection
- Curse Washed Away
- Candle Pentagram
- Stay Away
- Black Binding
- Broken Shards

Passion On Your Doorstep

Supplies:

- Three drops hot pepper sauce
- Three drops lavender oil
- Whole peppercorns
- Orris root slices
- Some Rosemary
- Three cups of rain water

The exact amount of herbs aren't important, as long as you have a little bit of each one in somewhat even proportions. Just a few pinches is fine. Put everything together in a bowl and stir. Think about the heat of the peppers, and the passion you want to enter into your life.

Sprinkle the water around on your doorstep, with your fingertips. Not just the step, but flick your fingers to spray a bit on the frame and walkway too.

When you are done, make sure to wash your hands. Even a little hot pepper sauce in the eyes will hurt.... and... erm... other areas.

Double Poppet

Poppets are common in many forms of Voodoo magic, and this spell will help you find the love of your life.

- Two pieces of Adam and Eve root
- One black poppet
- One red poppet
- Catnip

- Vervain

- Red and black string or yarn

For the herbs, you just need a few pinches of each. You have to make a small felt or cloth figure that you can stuff, one in black and one in red. They don't need to be very large. As you make them, put one piece of Adam and Eve root in each one and some of the other herbs. Make sure they are sew tightly shut so the herbs don't leak out.

Place the two poppets together, and tie them once with red yarn and once with black. Place this charm in your window during the night of the full moon, and leave it there until the next full moon. Love will soon come knocking.

Money Enchantment

You can bring extra cash into your life with this Voodoo spell for. Gather up the following items:

- A sheet of paper money

- A Needle and some red thread

- One piece of red cloth larger than the bill

- Some Coarse salt... at least a cup

- Some Pink candles

- Some Orange oil

- Amber incense

Gently use the needle and thread to sew the dollar bill onto the red cloth. Hang it up on wall, where you can set up the rest of your spell under it.

On a table or an altar, sprinkle a solid line of salt to make a square. Sit a candle at each corner of the square and light them. Put a little open dish of orange oil in the center. Dip the end of your incense stick into the oil, then light it in a holder outside the square. Repeat these words out loud:

Pinned to my soul forever more

Accompany my spirit to every shore

I trade you up for different things

Return to my pockets, bring, bring, bring

Leave the candles and the incense burning for an hour, then snuff them out. Leaving everything set up, repeat the spell (lighting candles, incense, and words) again for the next 2 days at the same time. Within 15 days, you will have more money.

Make Me Well

For when you have an illness.

You need to have:

- Some Blue fabric
- A few handfuls of dried beans (any kind)
- 2 small white buttons
- A sheet of white paper

Cut the blue fabric in 2 pieces that are roughly shaped like a person. Sew it up like a usual voodoo doll. Make sure that the stitches are firm and tight because you're going to be filling the doll with beans.

Draw a cross on the paper and put it into the doll body with the beans. Titch it up well and fasten on the two white buttons where the eyes should be.

Keep the doll under your bed until your illness has gone.

Stand Tall

To help you gain courage and confidence and strength.

Supplies:

   3 wooden sticks (approx 8 inches long)

   Some heavy twine or rough string

   One sturdy nail

   One dried chili pepper

Branches or twigs are best, but you can use dowels or even ice lolly sticks if that's what you have on hand.

Use the twine to tie the sticks together in a rough A shape, with the cross-piece close to the top to create a shape that looks like a person.

Tie the chilli pepper to one leg and the nail to the other. Wrap all the limbs and head of your stick doll in twine a few more times. Stand the doll up somewhere important in your home where you can frequently see it. When you do, remind yourself to stand tall when you make your choices during the day.

Pour On Protection

A strong protection spell with elements of voodoo, to be used to block unwanted magic from coming to your home. Do this spell on the night of the new moon (dark moon). You'll need to have:

   One cups of pure water (rain is best)

   Some Black ink

Four or Five black whole peppercorns

A pinch of graveyard dirt

A splash of vodka

One red candle

Light the candle before you start. Mix everything together in a glass or ceramic bowl. Stir everything around with the index finger of your left hand. Call to the voodoo God Legba to protect your house.

Go to your front door and pour the mixture all over the steps or pathway coming up to the door.

Floor Wash Lover

Here is a recipe for making a floor wash to help bring a little new love into your life.

One quart of fresh rain water

Half of a fresh lime

Five drops of pure rose oil

One whole bay leaf

Several white mustard seeds

Mix everything together and let it sit for at least an hour. After that, wash the floor in your kitchen with this mixture... just rub down the entire floor. It will start to draw love for you as soon as it dries.

Romance Doll

This spell is used to make someone fall in love with you

Supplies:

- A doll to represent your desired lover
- Something personal from him or her
- Something personal of your own
- Three lengths of ribbon, in red, black and white
- Some Paper
- One red Pen
- One white candle

The doll can be carved wax, molded clay or sewn fabric. A hand-made doll is much more powerful than a shop-bought object, so take the time to get it right. Add in the items from their body, using hairs, nail clippings or at least a bit of fabric from clothing they have worn. Also use the same items from yourself. Write or carve his or her name into the doll too.

Perform this spell on the day following the new moon. Set up an altar and light your candle. Wrap the doll in each piece of ribbon, knotting each one when necessary to keep it firm.

Say out loud:

Ribbons bind, forever entwine

My heart be yours and yours be mine

Write your love's name on the paper and leave it on the altar. Sit the doll on the paper and put out the candle. The next night, light the candle again and pick up the doll.

Very lightly and very carefully run the feet of the doll near to the flame... and say:

For you my heart yearns

For me your heart burns

Again, sit the doll on the paper. Now leave the candle burning for at least an hour. The person you desire will soon start to show some interest. When your spell is successful, wrap up the doll and put it somewhere safe to keep the attraction going.

Root Of Love

This variation on a rootwork spell will draw someone to you for some loving. It's particularly potent if you're after added passion as well as romance. You'll need:

One large piece of St. John the Conquerer root

Some Black thread

Some Red thread

Some Strands of your hair

Some Strands of your subject's hair

A Ceramic dish filled with dirt

One red candle

Wrap the piece of root with the hair, and then wrap it further with the red and black thread. Place the tied root charm in the bowl, and cover it over with dirt.

Ignite the red candle and hold it over the dish. Let several drops of red wax drop onto the dirt over the root... set the candle back up in a candle holder and let it continue burning.

After one week, your desired love will start to show serious interest in you.

Light Of Love

Supplies:

   Some red candles in the shape of a man and a woman

   Some "Come to Me" oil

   A large red dish or platter to hold both candles

If your local shop doesn't carry Come to Me oil, use a mix of patchouli and vanilla oils with a pinch of saffron.

Write your name in the wax of one candle, and the subject of your spell in the other. If you aren't after anyone particular, write "beloved be mine" instead.

Anoint both candles in the oil, and stand them in a large dish, close enough to touch. Light the candle representing you first, and then the other one. Simply say:

By the power of all the spirits

Bring my love to my arms

Leave the candles to burn out.

Bad Luck Locked In

Supplies:

   One solid padlock

   One sheet of paper

   Something sharp like a skewer

   Some Black paint

Write your enemy's name on a piece of paper and fold it once. Pierce the paper through the center to make a hole. Put the shaft of the lock through the hole and lock it.

Brush a blob of black paint over the keyhole and on either side of the lock. Hold the lock by the shaft until it dries, while repeating the following:

With this black lock

I send dark luck

With this spell,

You'll be struck.

Now bury the lock somewhere in your yard, and bury the key as close to your target's home as possible.

In The Dead of Night

This is a real black magic spell specifically designed to bring nightmares to another person. Cast this spell after midnight but before dawn.

Supplies:

One black candle

Some Mugwort

Some Dragon's blood resin

A Charcoal tablet

A Heat-proof dish

A Large piece of white paper or cloth

Some black ink (but a marker will do)

On the paper/cloth, drawn three concentric circles and an x in the center. Set the dish and charcoal on the x, and the candle outside the circles. Light the charcoal and get it smoldering, put a pinch of mugwort on it along with a chunk of the resin. When they are both smoking, light your candle.

As the smoke swirls up from the dish, visualize it floating through space to your intended target. It brings fear and nightmares to their slumber... picture that scene for several minutes while focusing on the individual.

After a few moments, extinguish the charcoal and switch the dish and candle so the candle is on the x. Leave it until it fully burns down. Your victim will have bad dreams starting the next night and it will last for three days.

Apple Sweet Enchantment

Supplies:

- One apple... preferably a red one
- Some Honey
- A few strands of your hair
- A few strands of your potential lover's hair
- A Length of red ribbon or yarn

Slice the apple sideways across the middle, so you can see the star shape made by the seeds. Spread honey on both of the apple halves. Take the strands of hair, and twist or braid them together.

Put the hairs between the two halves, and tie the apple back together with the ribbon. Tie it tightly. Bury the apple either outside, or in a large flower pot (outside is best). You'll find your desired lover start to show a strong interest in you almost immediately.

Your Heart be Mine

Turn someone's heart towards you...

Supplies:

- Two pink candles
- Two white candles
- One sheet of paper
- A Red marker
- Some Jasmine or Ylang Ylang oil

Firstly, run yourself a bath. At each corner of the bath, light the candles.

Then on the piece of paper, draw a big heart with the marker and put your name and your true love's name in the center... then draw a larger heart around the first one.

Rub a drop of the oil into each corner of the paper, then fold it into quarters. Hold the folded paper in your hands and repeat the two names out loud several times. Don't unfold the paper, but tear it into small pieces. Drop the pieces into the bath.

Now get in the bath, swishing the water around to help dissolve the paper, and rub the pieces on your body while you soak. Stay in the bath until the paper is completely broken down.

The Joining Of Two Spell

The photos you use shouldn't have anyone else in them except for you and him/her.

Supplies:

- A Photo of you
- A Photo of your desired
- One Red candle

- A marker pen

On the back of the photo of him/her, write "I love you" and on the back of your photo, write "You love me". Light the candle and look at both photos, picturing the two of you together in real life. Drip candle wax on the front sides of both photos and quickly stick them together.

Repeat the following:

Likeness of my myself

Likeness of my love

Bring us close forever more

We fit just like a glove

Slip the pair of photos under your pillow, and sleep with them there until your desired one is yours.

Boiling Rage

Boiling water will help you harness your emotional energy into a potent curse.

- A Cooking pot
- One a cup of water
- A few tablespoons of rock salt
- Any dead flower blossom
- A small jar or vial with a lid

Get the water boiling on the stove, and throw in the salt (save some for later).

Repeat the following:

Simmering power

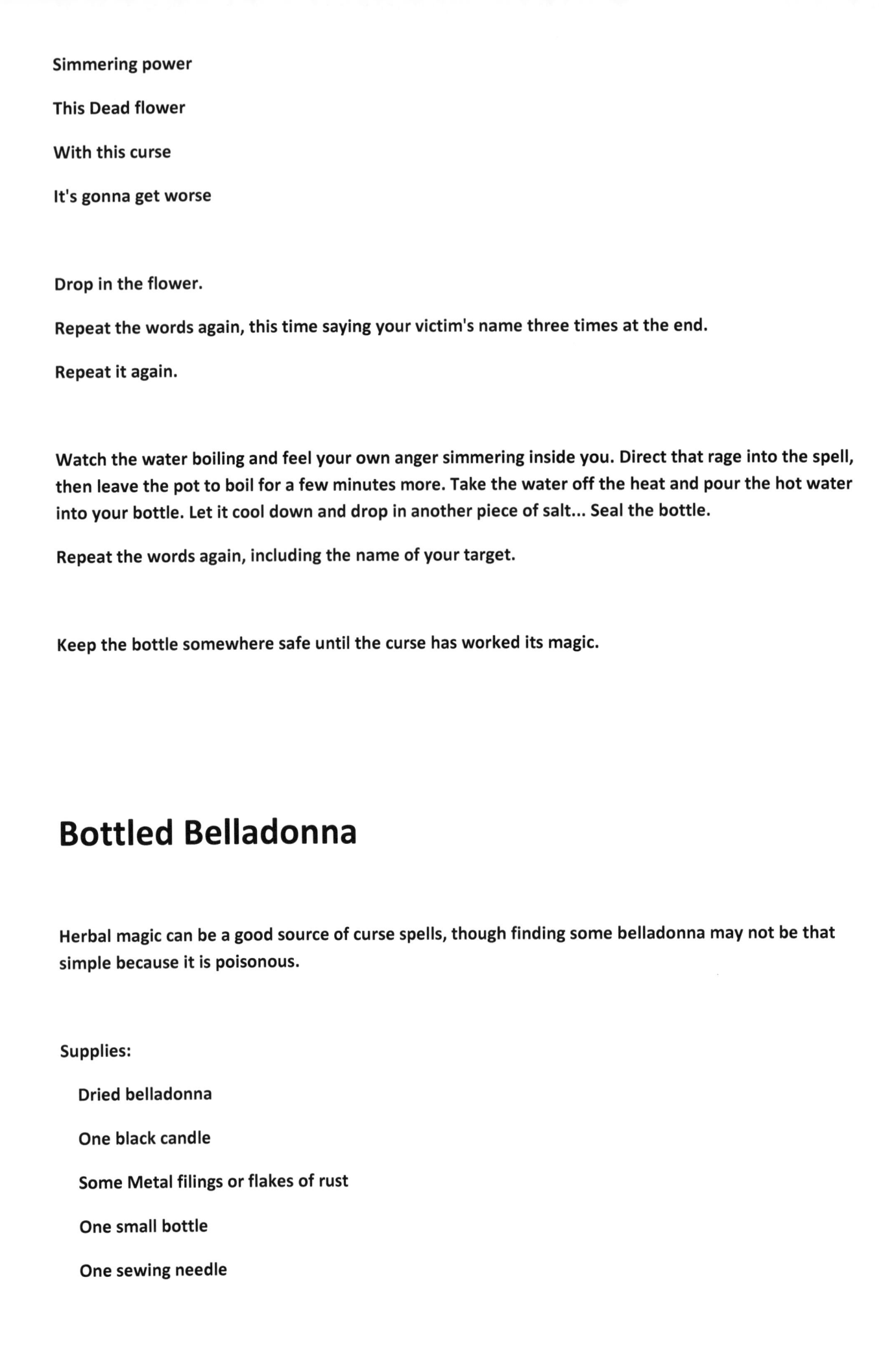

This Dead flower

With this curse

It's gonna get worse

Drop in the flower.

Repeat the words again, this time saying your victim's name three times at the end.

Repeat it again.

Watch the water boiling and feel your own anger simmering inside you. Direct that rage into the spell, then leave the pot to boil for a few minutes more. Take the water off the heat and pour the hot water into your bottle. Let it cool down and drop in another piece of salt... Seal the bottle.

Repeat the words again, including the name of your target.

Keep the bottle somewhere safe until the curse has worked its magic.

Bottled Belladonna

Herbal magic can be a good source of curse spells, though finding some belladonna may not be that simple because it is poisonous.

Supplies:

Dried belladonna

One black candle

Some Metal filings or flakes of rust

One small bottle

One sewing needle

Light the black candle and watch the flame for a few minutes while the wax begins to melt. Focus your thoughts on your victim and why you want to place this curse spell on them.

Put some rust or metal in the bottom of the bottle along with the belladonna, and then drop in the needle.

Pick up the candle and drip some wax into the bottle. Try to fill it at least a third full. It should cover over all the contents to keep it all in place... Say the words "Poison you" five times and put the lid on the bottle.

Bury the charm in your yard and it should start to work within a few days.

Covet Candle

Does someone elsehave something that you want? This spell is designed to make them lose it and have it come to you instead.

Supplies:

   One dark green candle

   Some hot red pepper flakes

   Two images of the object you want

   A fire-proof dish

You can use photos from newspapers or magazines, or draw them yourself. It doesn't have to be an exact photo of the object.

Put the two images together, face to face, with some of the red pepper flakes between them. Fold the pages in half, then in half again. Be sure to make sure the flakes stay inside the paper.

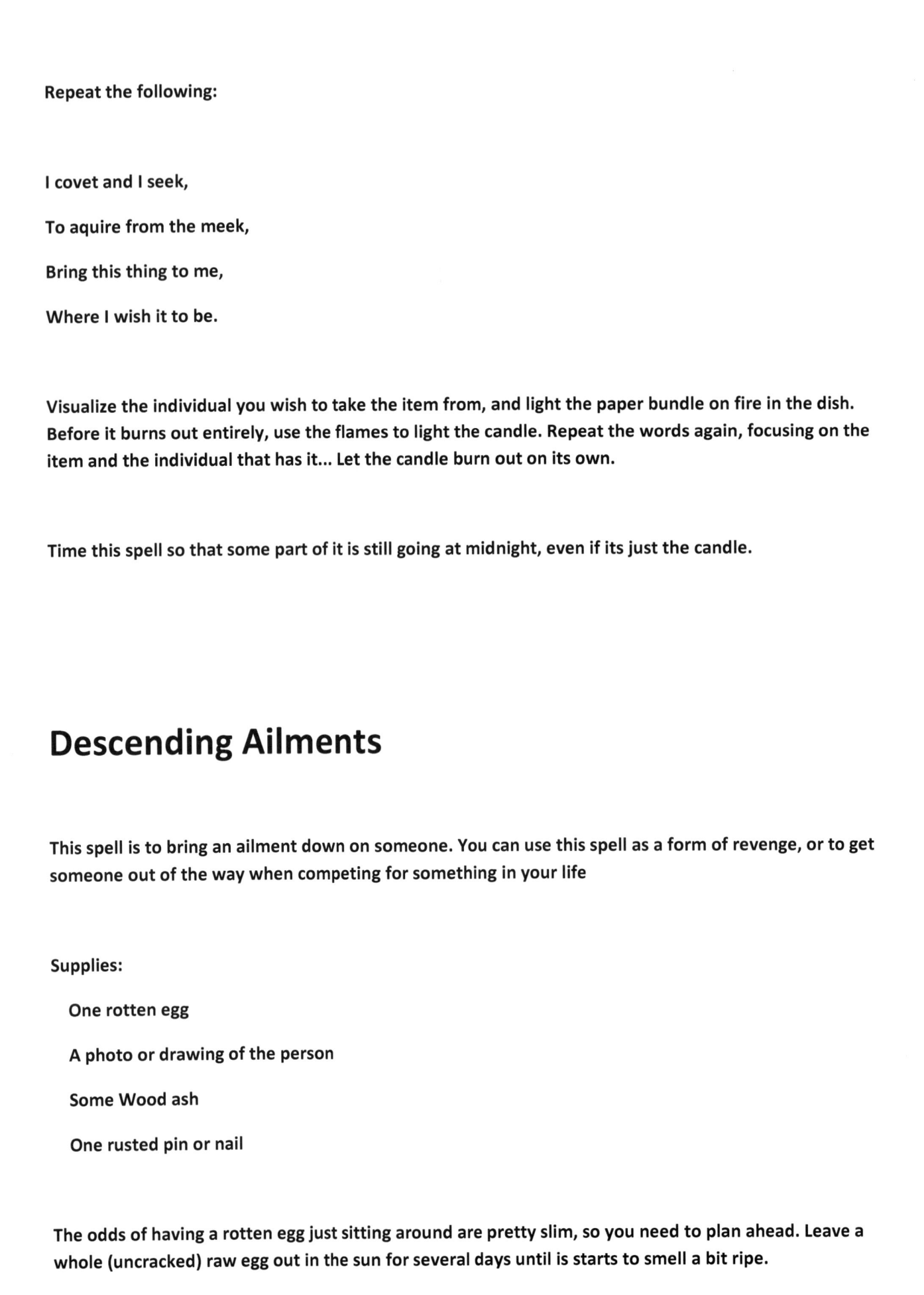

Repeat the following:

I covet and I seek,

To aquire from the meek,

Bring this thing to me,

Where I wish it to be.

Visualize the individual you wish to take the item from, and light the paper bundle on fire in the dish. Before it burns out entirely, use the flames to light the candle. Repeat the words again, focusing on the item and the individual that has it... Let the candle burn out on its own.

Time this spell so that some part of it is still going at midnight, even if its just the candle.

Descending Ailments

This spell is to bring an ailment down on someone. You can use this spell as a form of revenge, or to get someone out of the way when competing for something in your life

Supplies:

  One rotten egg

  A photo or drawing of the person

  Some Wood ash

  One rusted pin or nail

The odds of having a rotten egg just sitting around are pretty slim, so you need to plan ahead. Leave a whole (uncracked) raw egg out in the sun for several days until is starts to smell a bit ripe.

When you are intending to do this spell, remember that it will smell real nasty, so you might not want other people around atthe time.

Sit the photo on a plate. Pierce the egg with the rusted pin and crack it open over the photograph. Let the mess cover the picture as you think about the target getting sick. Sprinkle some wood ash over the rotten egg. Let everything sit for a few minutes. Again, concentrate on your intentions as you enjoy the 'aroma'.

Then take the plate outside and bury the whole mess with the picture facing downwards.

Your victim will be ill within a week.

Reflect Your Revenge

Mirrors are extremely powerful in returning energy back to someone, and are ideal for revenge spells like this.

Supplies:

  One small mirror

  A Black permanent marker

  A Long piece of black ribbon

  One Whole bay leaf

  Some Burnt wood ash

Cast this spell on a Saturday night.

First write the target's name on the face of the mirror is big letters, then set the bay leaf over the name. Wrap the mirror and leaf in the ribbon a few times and then add a generous pinch of ash over the leaf. Wrap a few more times and then tie with a good solid knot.

Place one hand on either side of the mirror... and say:

From me to you,

Return times two.

Keep the wrapped up mirror charm under your bed, until you feel that your vengeance has happened. Don't leave it forever though... Once some bad luck has fallen on your adversary, remove it and destroy the spell.

Black Moon Revenge

Perform this spell on a new moon.

- One black candle
- A Sharp tool to scribe the candle (such small, flat screwdriver)
- A Piece of onyx or jet

Carve the name of your target into the candle and sit it in a candle holder. Focus on this person wronged you, and watch the flame burn. When the candle has melted down enough to start melting where you wrote their name, take it out of the holder and let several drops of wax fall over the stone.

While the wax is still soft, mark the person's first initial into the wax then let it cool and set. Let the candle finish burning down and leave the stone in a safe place until your revenge has happened. Bury the stone in the earth.

Peppered Pentacle

This is a general spell to cause bad luck or misfortune to fall on a foe.

Supplies:

   A White sheet of paper

   Some black pepper

   A Pen

   One Black candle

Draw a large pentacle on the paper. Write your victim's name in the center. Sprinkle a fine line of pepper around the outline of the pentacle. Now light the candle and let it burn for a few minutes to get the wax melting.

Hold the candle over the pentacle and let it drip onto the person's name... enough to cover the writing. Let the candle burn for an hour before extinguishing it. Leave your pepper sigil in place where it won't be disturbed until your spell takes effect.

Curse Of The Rocky Road

This is a bad luck spell that you can use to target anyone in your life, even if you don't have any details about them.

   A gnarly rock (roughly fist sized)

   Some black paint

   A slip of paper

   A length of black yarn or ribbon

   One whole dry bay leaf

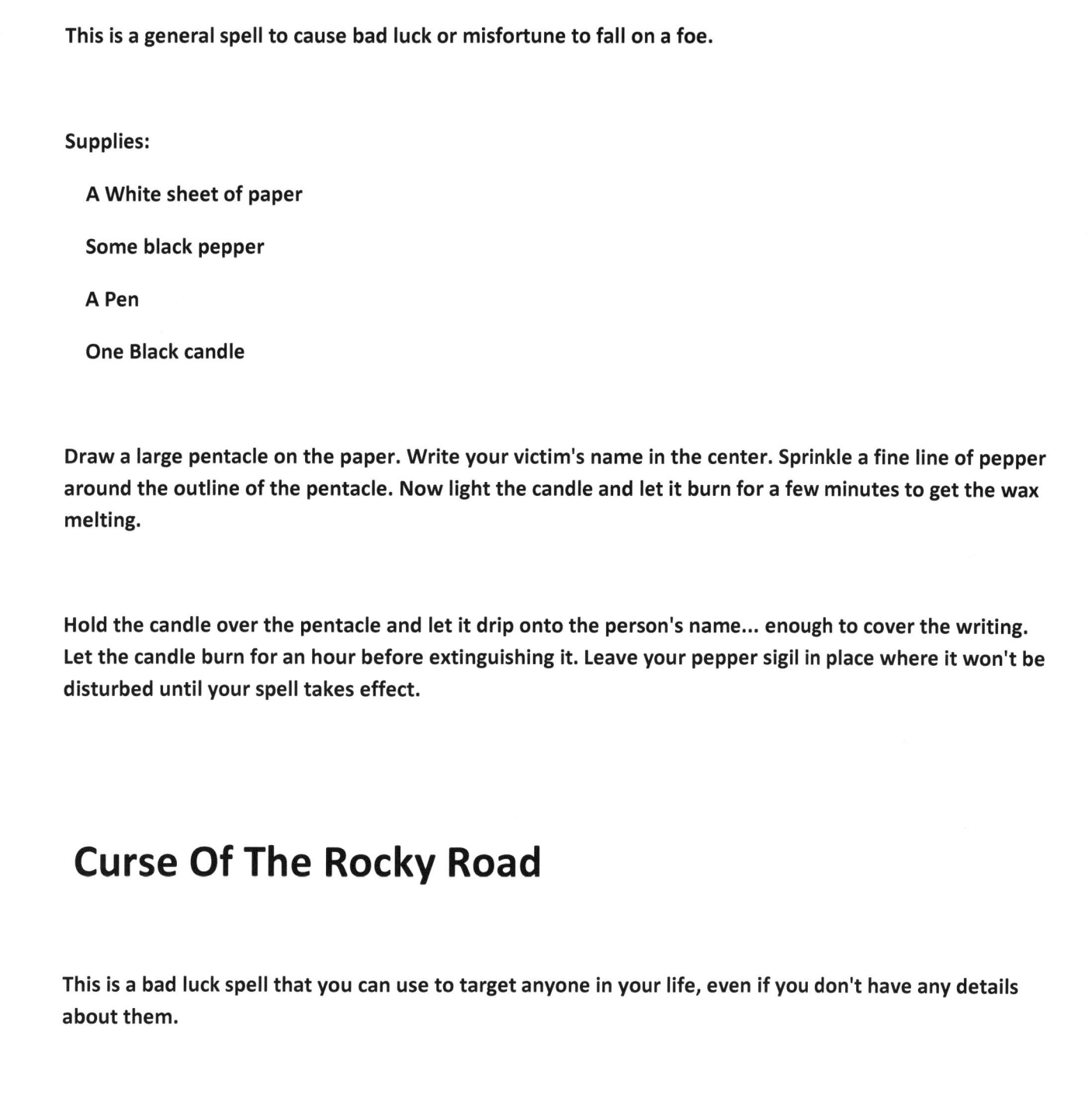

Paint the entire rock black and let it dry.

Write your intended victim's name on the piece of paper. Fold the paper over once and tie it to the rock along with the bay leaf. The paper should be touching the stone. Tie the string with a knot.

Put the stone in a dark place so that it's sitting on the piece of paper. Give the spell three days to start taking effect, and your chosen person will start having quite a lot of bad luck.

Snake Eyes

Unexpected bad luck will show up for someone after doing this spell.

Supplies:

- A pair of dice
- Some black pepper

Dig a hole several inches deep inyour yard. Set the dice at the bottom, with the one's facing upwards. Cover them over with the pepper and repeat the following:

Your luck is running out,

You'll be in a hole.

Bad things will happen,

That is my goal.

Focus your mind on the person you are sending this spell to... then fill the hole in with soil. Stamp it down well, then just leave it to make its magic.

Dark Embrace

Get to know your darker side with this ritual, performed on the night of a new moon.

Supplies:

   A dark bowl

   Some Black ink

   One sharp pin

   Some black pepper

   One black candle

On the night of a new moon the sky is extremely dark, and the perfect time to tap into darker forces. Light the candle and place it as far away from you as you can whilst still being able to see what you're doing... basically work in shaddow.

Fill the bowl with water, then add nine drops of the black ink. Wait a few moments for the darkness to spread through the water. Sprinkle some pepper onto the surface of the water.

Now speak the words:

Shadows dark, spirits within

Harness the energy, let us begin

Draw powers from the moon

Harness the tides

I need to embrace

My sinister side

Now prick your finger with the pin and let a drop of blood fall into the water.

Speak the words again.

Take the bowl outside and dump it all out into the ground. You'll soon start to feel new connection to your darker shadow spirit.

Shaddow Whispers

This is a summoning spell to address the very nature of the shadow.

A large mirror

A piece of black cloth large enough to cover the mirror

Some patchouli incense

A black marker, or paint

Use the marker or paint to draw Theban symbols in the four corners of the mirror. Lean your forehead to touch the middle of the mirror for a few seconds, feeling the cool glass. Light the incense and drape fabric over the mirror.

Touch each of the four corners and then immediately rip away the cloth. At that moment, you'll get a strong impression or even see a message in the mirror from the shadow.

Banishing Mirror

This spell directs someone's vision back towards themselves, making you invisible to them.

Supplies:

A small mirror

A Photo or drawing of the person

A Piece of onyx

A pinch of mugwort

Put the mirror flat on a table and sprinkle a pinch of mugwort in one spot on the face of the mirror. Lay the photo face-down on the mirror so the face of the person is over the mugwort.

Speak the following words:

   You can't see me

   You can't hear me

   You can't feel me

   Your attention leaves me

Now set the onyx on top of the photograph, also over where the persons face.

Speak the words again and leave the items on your altar to keep this person away.

For the most powerful effect, cast this spell on the night of the new moon.

Freeze Out Your Foe

Another classic banishing technique is to freeze someone to make them powerless against you.

Supplies:

One small sheet of paper

A black pen

One small piece of black string

Some Water

A freezer

On the piece of paper, write the name of the person you want to banish. Tie a single knot in the middle of the string, and focus on why this person is bothering you whilst you tie it.

Fold the paper up, with the piece of string tucked into the middle. Add a few drops of water to the paper. Place the wet, folded paper in the freezer and leave there until the situation is solved.

The Banishing Jar

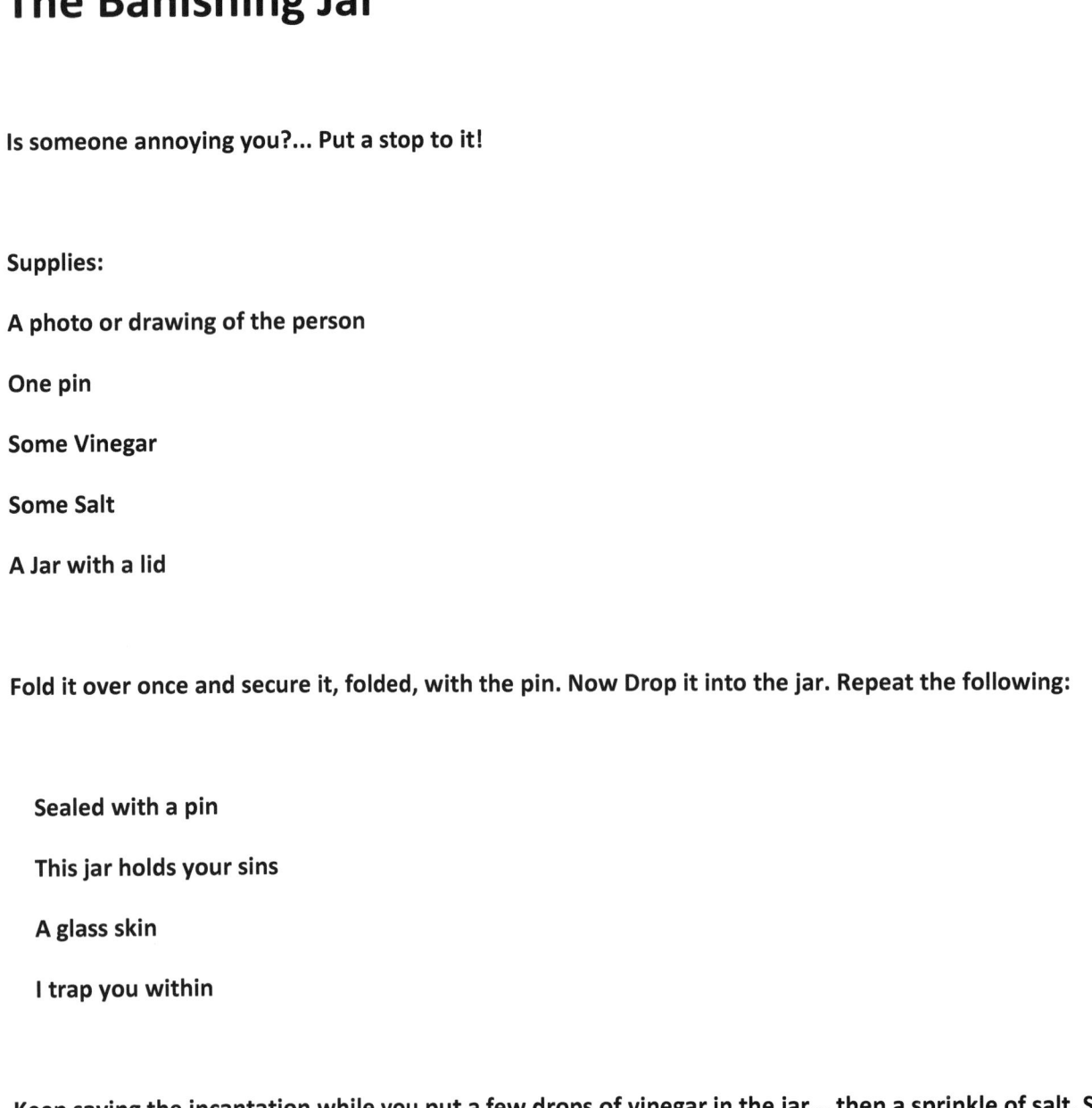

Is someone annoying you?... Put a stop to it!

Supplies:

A photo or drawing of the person

One pin

Some Vinegar

Some Salt

A Jar with a lid

Fold it over once and secure it, folded, with the pin. Now Drop it into the jar. Repeat the following:

> Sealed with a pin
>
> This jar holds your sins
>
> A glass skin
>
> I trap you within

Keep saying the incantation while you put a few drops of vinegar in the jar... then a sprinkle of salt. Seal the lid tightly and put the jar in a dark place.

The Witch Bottle

This is a classic spell to protect your home.

Supplies:

A jar with a tight lid

Some pieces of broken glass

Some nails, or pins (rusty is best)

A pinch of dried rosemary and/or rue

Some Vinegar

The exact amount of any items will depend a lot on how big a jar you use.

Fill the jar with broken glass, rusty nails/pins. Fill the rest of the jar with vinegar.

Seal the jar tightly and bury it just outside your front door.

A witch bottle will protect your house for years.

Home Security

Seal your home up from any unwelcome and negative influences.

Supplies:

- A small handful of coarse salt
- A teaspoon or so of garlic powder

Stir the salt and garlic together and put a few pinches of it on every windowsill and doorway in your house.

Both salt and garlic are potent protective magick.

Herbal Shield

This spell is intended to add protection to you personally.

The exact amounts of the herbs are up to you.

Supplies:

Rosemary

Rue

Lavender

Basil

Mint

A handful of coarse salt

Run a hot bath and throw in all your ingrediants. Let the bath sit for a few minutes before getting in. Sit and soak for a while, visualizing that your body is picking up protective energy from the water.

When you're finished, save a bit of the water and herbs in a bowl and throw it outside.

Deflect Harm

Supplies:

Two small mirrors

One black candle

Some Sandalwood incense

Light the incense and let the smoke build up around your altar. Carve a deep X into the candle.

You now have to set up your two mirrors so they face each other (so mirrors with stands would be best) and place the candle between them. It should look like repeating candles reflected deep within the mirror.

Light the candle, and let your eyes focus back and forth between the mirrors while you concentrate on the negative magic you are trying to reverse.

Say the words:

   Magic against me

   Entrapped this night

   Betwixt these mirrors

   Banashed from light

Repeat the chant over and over again, visualizing the curse becoming entangled in the reflections and sent back from whence it came. Let the candle burn down on its own, but leave the mirrors facing each other for one month.

Reversing Vinegar

Supplies:

Some Pure white vinegar

Several pinches of fennel seed

A small white bowl

One piece of jet or onyx

The day before you plan on doing this spell, pour an ounce or two of vinegar into the bowl and add some fennel seed. Let this sit and "steep" until the next day.

On the next night, dip your fingers in the vinegar and dab a little bit on each wrist, your throat and your forehead. Just a little on the forehead because you don't want vinegar dripping in your eyes.

Sit with your eyes closed, and visualize white energy pushing out from your body at this points and forcing the negative magick back towards the sender. Force it away from you. When you are done, place the stone in the bowl, and leave it for 5 days. After that, pour the vinegar away into the ground.

Psychic Shield

This charm bag is a potent Wiccan spell that will protect against psychic attacks.

Supplies:

Four black candles

A small black fabric bag

A tablespoon of Anise

A tablespoon of Horehound

A tablespoon of Sandalwood

A tablespoon of Rue

A small piece of Onyx

A small piece of Jet

A small piece of Hematite

Before you use it, you need to assemble and charge up this protection charm. Set the four candles up in a square. In the centre, pile all the parts of your charm bag. Light the candles and focus on their light.

Visualize it flowing into the center and filling up the herbs and stones you have there.

Speak the following words:

By the light of these four,

You'll harm me no more.

Repeat several times while you charge up the materials. When you're happy, gather everything together and fill the bag with the stones and herbs. Tie it tightly and place it back in the center of the candles. Do the same visualization and repeat the same words again. When you feel that the bag is ready to go, put out the candles and carry the charm with you everywhere.

Unbreakable Shell Spell

This will create a protective "shield" around an object, protecting it from intrusion or theft.

Supplies

- The item you want to protect
- Five pieces of obsidian
- Three feet of black yarn
- Some ground rosemary

Set your item on a table, and place the five pieces of stone in a pentagram shape around the object. Start to imagine a shell being formed over your item.

Use the piece of string to lay out a pentacle, using the stones at the points of the star.

When the star is done, say out loud:

With line unbroken,

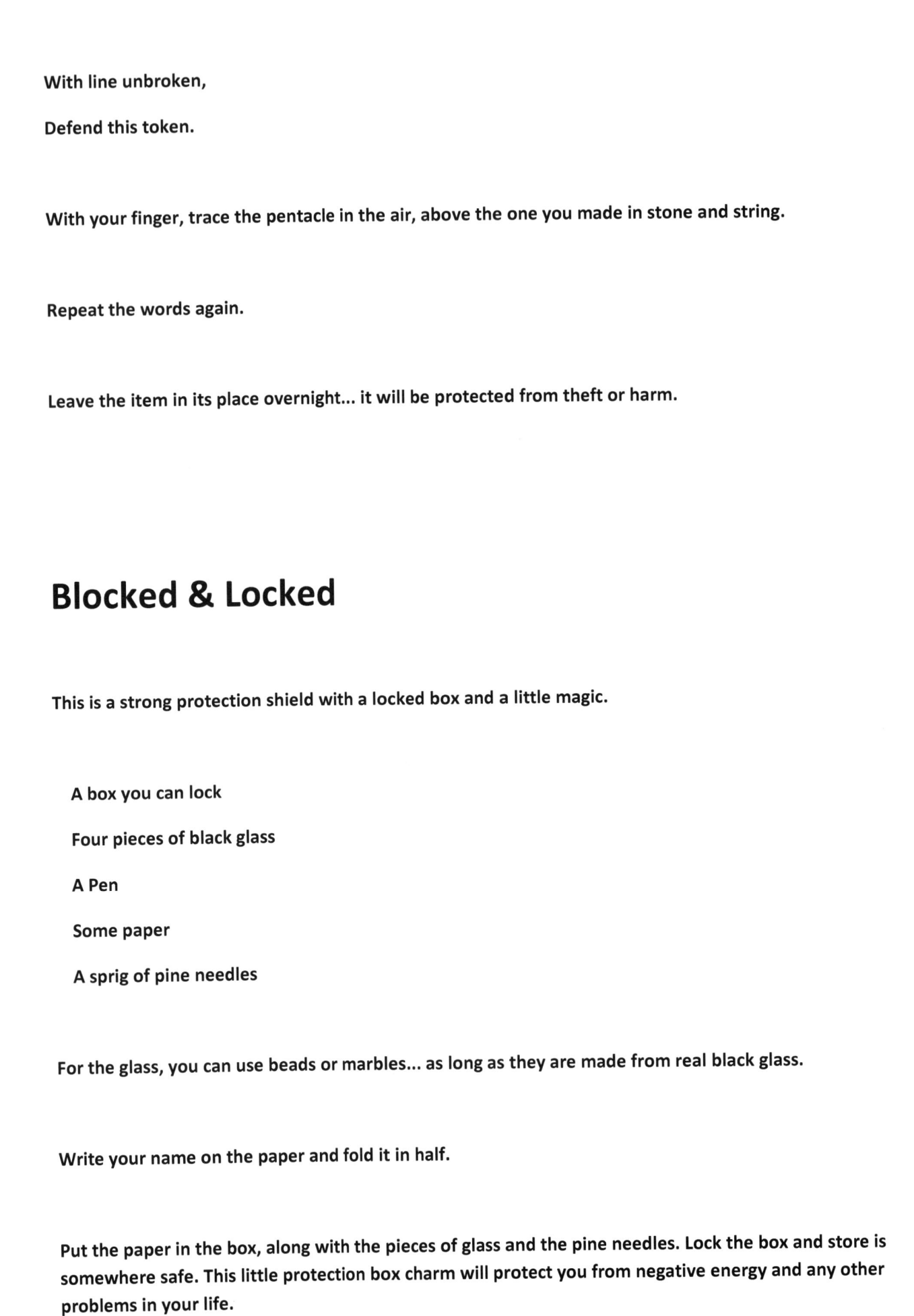

Defend this token.

With your finger, trace the pentacle in the air, above the one you made in stone and string.

Repeat the words again.

Leave the item in its place overnight... it will be protected from theft or harm.

Blocked & Locked

This is a strong protection shield with a locked box and a little magic.

- A box you can lock
- Four pieces of black glass
- A Pen
- Some paper
- A sprig of pine needles

For the glass, you can use beads or marbles... as long as they are made from real black glass.

Write your name on the paper and fold it in half.

Put the paper in the box, along with the pieces of glass and the pine needles. Lock the box and store is somewhere safe. This little protection box charm will protect you from negative energy and any other problems in your life.

Deflection Reflection

This is another mirror spell that will reflect difficulties away from you.

Supplies:

A wall-mounted mirror

A black crayon or marker

Use a mirror that you see or use often.

Draw a pentacle in the top left corner, at least as large as your hand.

Press your thumb to the glass at each point of the star, leaving five fingerprints around the pentacle.

Every day, when you look at the mirror, touch the center of the star to refresh the spell and bounce away any evil intentions set against you.

Curse Washed Away

Supplies:

Twelve white candles

One black candle

One cup of coarse salt

One tablespoon of lavender blossoms

One tablespoon of white sage

One tablespoon of chamomile

You can be liberal with the herbs, as long as they are in roughly the same proportions.

Envoke this spell on the night after a full moon. On your altar, make a circle with the twelve white candles. Put the black one in the middle... Don't light them just yet.

Run a warm bath and add the salt and the herbs. Light the candles and get into the bath.

Get comfortable and repeat the following:

   By the sacred moon's peaceful wane

   Cleanse my souland cleanse this stain

   Let this spell be reversed

   Banish to darkness, banish this curse

   As I sit within my sacred space

   Free my soul and bring me grace

Pour some of the bathwater over your head (keeping your eyes closed). Do this 3 times and say these words each time:

   I now forgive all that was done

   Let this curse that's been cursing me be gone

Stay in the bath tub until the water begins to cool. When you get out, snuff out the candles but leave them in their places. For the next three nights relight them all and repeat the second part of the chant. After the third night, relight the black candle and let it burn all the way out to nothing.

Candle Pentagram

You'll need to set this breaking spell out on a table that won't be disturbed for the duration.

Supplies:

Salt

Five white candles

Some Rosemary

Sprinkle a fine line of salt to draw a pentacle on your table. It doesn't have to be perfect, but try to get it somewhat symmetrical. Add some rosemary to each point of the star... Then set one white candle at each point.

Light each candle, starting with the one at the top.

After each one, say the words:

   By darkness and light

   Your spell ends tonight

Let the candles burn for one hour, then put them out. Do the same thing the next time, except let them burn all the way down.

Leave the candle stubs in place for another five days, so the entire spell is in place for a whole week. After that, any negative magic against you will be gone.

Stay Away!

This is one of the most simple binding spells, often used to keep someone away who is pestering you. Be it an annoying co-worker or a creepy ex. It doesn't really stop any specific action, just keeps them out of your life.

Supplies:

A piece of cardboard

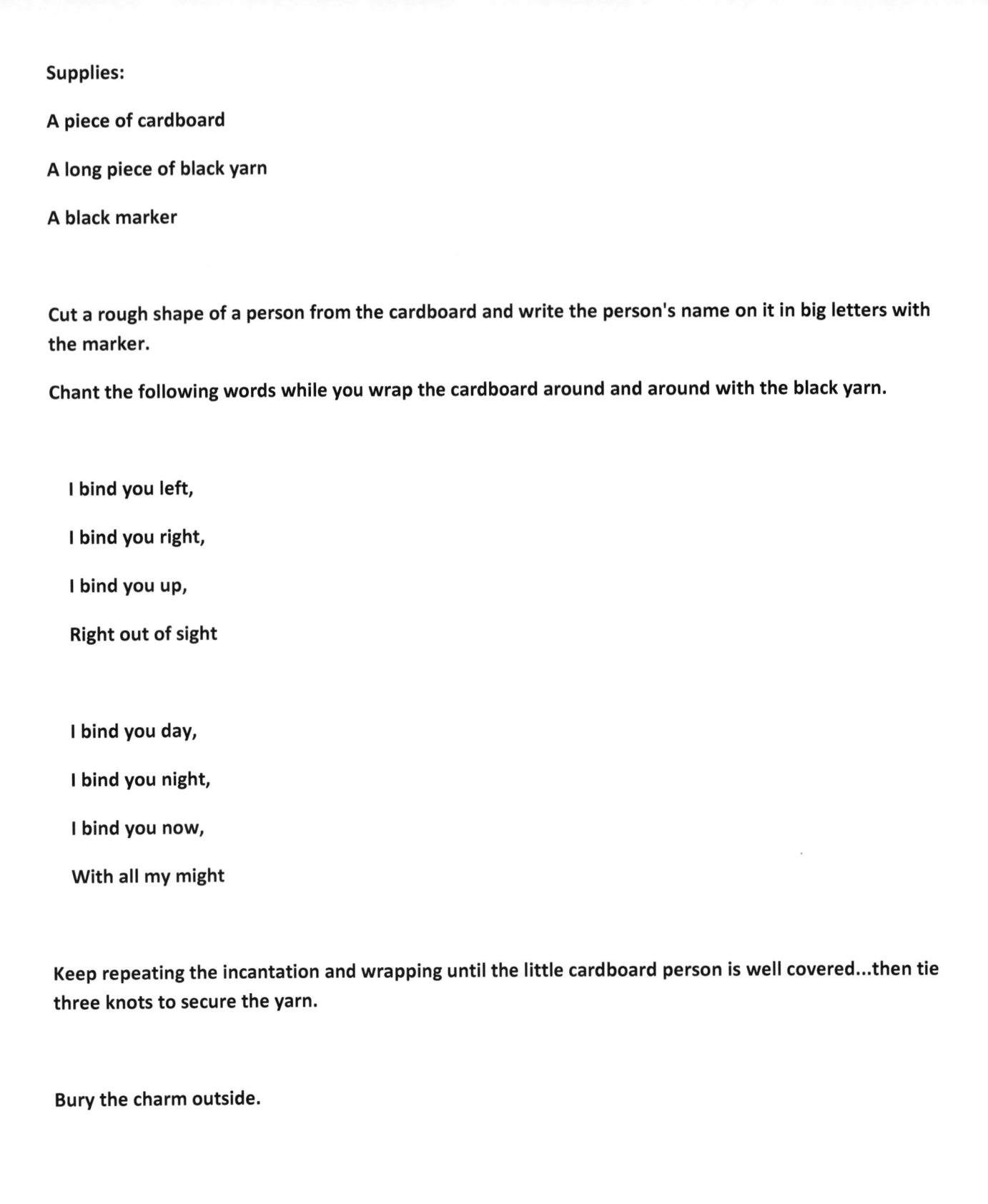

A long piece of black yarn

A black marker

Cut a rough shape of a person from the cardboard and write the person's name on it in big letters with the marker.

Chant the following words while you wrap the cardboard around and around with the black yarn.

    I bind you left,

    I bind you right,

    I bind you up,

    Right out of sight

    I bind you day,

    I bind you night,

    I bind you now,

    With all my might

Keep repeating the incantation and wrapping until the little cardboard person is well covered...then tie three knots to secure the yarn.

Bury the charm outside.

Black Binding

Another great binding spell.

One black candle

A length of rough twine

A length of black yarn

A length of black thread

Some sandalwood oil

The exact lengths of the twine, yarn and thread doesn't matter, just use the same for all three.

Anoint the candle with the sandalwood oil while you focus your mind on the person you want to remove from your life. Wrap the black thread around the candle until you use the whole length, then tie it tightly. Then the yarn, and then the twine on top of that.

Light the candle, letting it burn out completely. Keep it somewhere safe and flameproof because the strings might catch fire as the candle burns down.

Shattered Glass

This charm bag is carried around with you at all times to protect you from the effects of a negative spell

Supplies:

    A small black bag made of a sturdy fabric

    Three shards of broken glass

    One piece of onyx

    A piece of copper wire about three inches long

Twist up the bit of wire into a knot and drop it into the bag, saying:

"You are broken and have no power over me".

Repeat these words as you drop each piece of glass and the stone into the bag. Tie the bag tightly... also repeating the same words.

Now you need to have this bag with you for 7 days, including near your bed when you are sleeping.

Printed in Great Britain
by Amazon